MONEY MASTERY: 7 SIMPLE STEPS TO TAKE CONTROL OF YOUR FINANCES

DINESH SHARMA ARYAL

Made with ♥ on the Notion Press Platform
www.notionpress.com

Dear Readers,

My name is Dinesh Sharma Aryal, and I am a financial professional with over 16 years of experience in the banking, insurance, and financial services sectors. I am thrilled to present to you my very first book, which I wholeheartedly dedicate to you—my readers.

In today's fast-paced world, most people are caught up in their daily responsibilities, working tirelessly to support themselves and their families. However, many often overlook the importance of proper financial and investment planning to achieve their life goals.

This book is a humble effort to provide you with a simple and practical understanding of financial planning. I sincerely hope that after reading it, you will gain clarity on how to align your investments with your financial goals.

Thank you for your time and trust.

Warm regards,
Dinesh Sharma Aryal
Author

Contents

Foreword

In a world where financial uncertainty is constant and opportunities are ever-changing, having a clear roadmap to navigate personal finance is no longer optional—it's essential.

This book by Dinesh Sharma Aryal, a seasoned financial expert with over 16 years of experience, offers a practical and relatable approach to understanding financial planning. Whether you're a salaried individual, a small business owner, or someone simply trying to manage your money better, this book presents core concepts in a straightforward and actionable way.

What sets this work apart is its real-world relevance. Dinesh doesn't just talk theory—he draws from years of hands-on experience in banking, insurance, and financial institutions to give you insights that actually work in real life.

This book is a must-read for anyone who is ready to take control of their financial future.

Preface

The idea for this book was born out of the countless conversations I've had over the years with clients, friends, and colleagues—many of whom were hard-working individuals struggling with the basics of financial planning.

Despite earning well, many people fail to structure their finances effectively and miss out on the opportunity to secure their future. I realized that there was a clear need for a simple, jargon-free guide that speaks directly to the everyday person.

This book is not intended to be an academic manual filled with complex formulas. Instead, it is a practical guide to help you understand your financial needs, set clear goals, and take meaningful steps toward achieving them.

My goal is to equip you with the knowledge and confidence to make informed financial decisions that serve you and your family for years to come.

I hope this book becomes a valuable companion in your financial journey.

— Dinesh Sharma Aryal

Acknowledgements

First and foremost, I thank God for giving me the strength, patience, and clarity to complete this book.

I am deeply grateful to my family, especially my [mention wife, parents, or children, if you'd like], for their unwavering support and belief in me throughout this journey.

A special thanks to my friends, mentors, and colleagues from the banking and finance world, who inspired and challenged me to think deeply about financial literacy and its real-world impact.

To my readers, thank you for choosing this book. Your trust means everything. I hope it empowers you to take smart financial steps in your life.

Lastly, I want to thank the team at Notion Press for providing this wonderful platform to bring my voice to life.

With heartfelt gratitude,
Dinesh Sharma Aryal

Prologue

Imagine standing at a crossroads in life—one road leads to financial stress and uncertainty, while the other leads to stability, growth, and freedom. The only difference between the two is knowledge.

Most of us are never taught how to manage money, set financial goals, or choose the right investment tools. We earn, we spend, and we hope for the best. But hope alone is not a strategy.

This book is designed to give you that missing knowledge. It's a roadmap to understanding money—not from a textbook perspective, but from real-world experience.

The goal isn't to turn you into a financial expert overnight, but to help you become financially aware, goal-oriented, and better prepared for the future.

Let's take the first step together toward building a secure and fulfilling financial life.

— Dinesh Sharma Aryal

CHAPTER ONE

INTRODUCTION: WHY FINANCIAL FREEDOM MATTERS

Most people work hard for money, but the wealthy make money work for them. Financial freedom isn't about being rich; it's about having peace of mind, choice, and security. When you control your finances, you control your life.

In this mini-guide, you will learn simple, actionable steps to help you master your money, reduce financial stress, and build lasting wealth.

What Is Financial Freedom?

Financial freedom means having enough income, savings, and assets to cover your lifestyle needs — without depending on a job or stressing over money. It's about control, choice, and peace of mind.

Why Financial Freedom Truly Matters ?

1. Freedom of Time

| "Time is the real wealth. Money just buys it."

- You're no longer exchanging hours for rupees.
- You can spend time with family, pursue hobbies, travel, or volunteer.

- You get to live life on your terms, not your employer's.

2. Freedom of Choice

- Want to say no to a toxic job? You can.
- Want to work part-time or take a break? You can.
- You're not forced into decisions just because you need the next paycheck.

3.Peace of Mind

- Emergency medical bills? Covered.
- Kids' education? Already planned.
- You sleep better knowing your future is financially secure.

4. Retirement Before 60

- Financial freedom allows you to retire early — even in your 40s or 30s.
- You can build passive income (e.g., rent, dividends, digital products).

5. Build Generational Wealth

- You not only live stress-free, but also leave behind assets for your children.
- True financial freedom creates a legacy, not just a lifestyle.

6. More Focus on Purpose, Not Paychecks

- You can start a passion project.
- You can help others through coaching, donations, or volunteering.
- You're driven by purpose, not money.

How to Start the Journey?

Start with:

- Budgeting and saving
- Investing wisely (mutual funds, stocks, insurance)
- Creating multiple income streams (side hustles, freelancing, etc.)

CHAPTER TWO

TRACK EVERY RUPEE

What Does "Track Every Rupee" Mean?

"Track Every Rupee" means **knowing exactly where every single rupee you earn, spend, save, or invest goes.**

It's not just a budgeting habit — it's a **mindset of money awareness.**

Why Is It So Important?

You can't control what you don't measure.

If your money keeps disappearing and you wonder **"Where did all my salary go?"**, that's a sign you're not tracking it.

The truth:

People don't go broke from one big expense.
They go broke from hundreds of small, ignored expenses.

Top 5 Benefits of Tracking Every Rupee

1. Reveals the Truth About Your Spending Habits

- You'll be shocked how much you spend on Zomato, mobile recharge, chai, etc.
- Tracking shows your real financial behavior vs. what you think you do.

2. Helps You Cut Waste

- Once you see ₹4,000/month going to impulse shopping, it's easy to cut back.
- You stop asking "Where did my money go?" and start saying "I know where it's going."

3. Boosts Your Savings Rate

- What gets measured improves.
- You'll start saving 20–30% of your income just by becoming aware.

4. Reduces Stress and Guilt

- No more guesswork or guilt after buying something.
- You'll be in control — not surprised by your bank balance.

5. Lays the Foundation for Wealth

- Whether you want to invest, start a side hustle, or build assets — tracking is Step 1.
- Even big investors and millionaires use expense trackers.

How to Track Every Rupee (Practically)?

1. Use a Notebook (Old-School Method)

- Write down every income and expense daily
- Create monthly summaries for clarity

2. Use Mobile Apps (Modern & Easy)

- **Walnut, Money Manager, Moneyfy, Spendee**, or even **Google Sheets**
- Categorize spending: Food, Rent, EMI, Entertainment, Fuel, etc.

3. Auto Alerts via SMS

- Many apps auto-read your SMS (securely) and track expenses
- You can check spending trends anytime

Final Thought:

"Every wealthy person started with one step: Knowing where their money goes."

CHAPTER THREE

BUDGET LIKE A PRO

What Does "Budget Like a Pro" Mean?

To "budget like a pro" means more than just writing down income and expenses. It's about **planning, prioritizing, and managing your money intentionally**, so every rupee works for your goals — not against them.

A professional budget is:

- Strategic
- Realistic
- Flexible
- Aligned with long-term goals

Why Do Most People Fail at Budgeting?

- They guess instead of tracking
- They create unrealistic plans
- They forget to adjust for real life
- They never follow up

But a pro budgeter?

Tracks, tweaks, and thrives.

How to Budget Like a Pro — Step-by-Step

1. Know Your Net Income

This is your **real take-home amount** after taxes, PF, EMI deductions, etc.
　Example:
　Monthly Salary = 　₹45,000
　After deductions = 　₹39,500 → That's your budget base

2. Use the 50-30-20 Rule (Starter Formula)

Category / Description / Example on ₹39,500
　50% Needs / Rent, groceries, bills, EMI / 　₹19,750
　30% Wants / Eating out, shopping, Netflix / 　₹11,850
　20% Savings or Investments / SIPs, insurance, FD / 　₹7,900
　| This rule keeps lifestyle & future in balance.

3. Break Expenses into Clear Categories

Fixed Expenses / Variable Expenses / Future Goals
　Rent, EMI, Bills / Food, Travel, Shopping / Emergency fund, SIP, FD
　Use Google Sheets, apps like **Walnut**, or paper journal.

4. Plan for the Unexpected

Budgeting like a pro includes:

- Emergency buffer (₹2K–₹5K/month)
- One-time spends: gifts, travel, insurance renewals

This avoids debt traps and broken budgets.

5. Automate Good Habits

| The pro doesn't rely on memory, he relies on systems.

- Set auto-debit for SIPs and RD
- Use reminders for bill payments
- Use budgeting apps to alert overspending

6. Review Weekly, Adjust Monthly

At the end of every week:

- Check how much you spent vs. planned
- Tweak your categories if needed
- Celebrate if you saved more than planned

Advanced Budgeting Tips (Pro Level)

Create multiple savings buckets:

- Emergency fund
- Travel fund
- Gadget fund (Use bank apps like Fi Money, Jupiter, or SBI YONO Goals)

Follow Zero-Based Budgeting:

- Every rupee has a job
- You end each month with ₹0 unassigned (not unspent)

Track spending triggers:

- Is it stress eating? Impulse sales? Online ads?
- Pro budgeting includes self-awareness

Remember This:

| "Budgeting is not about restrictions. It's about direction."

CHAPTER FOUR

Cut Expenses Without Feeling Deprived

What Does It Mean?

Cutting expenses **doesn't mean killing your joy** or living like a monk.
It means:

- Redirecting money from wasteful to meaningful
- Spending less on what doesn't matter
- So you can spend more (or save) on what truly does

When done smartly, **you won't even feel the pinch** — and you'll feel more in control.

Quote: "It's not your salary that makes you rich, it's your spending habits." – Charles A. Jaffe

Top 7 Ways to Cut Expenses Without Feeling Deprived

1. Audit Your Spending for Leaks

Start by tracking every rupee for 30 days (use apps or Google Sheets). You'll discover:

- Hidden subscriptions you forgot to cancel
- Multiple payments for similar services
- Daily habits draining your wallet (chai + snacks = ₹3,000/month?)

Action: Cancel or reduce anything you don't love or use often.

2. Embrace Smart Swaps

Cutting costs doesn't mean cutting enjoyment — it's about being clever.
Before / After
₹180 coffee at café every day / Brew at home: ₹20
₹800 on movie + snacks / OTT movie night at home
Branded grocery store / Local store or wholesale apps
Result: Same joy, less spend.

3. Unfollow Lifestyle Triggers

Much of our spending comes from comparison and temptation.
Unfollow:

- Influencers who promote excessive shopping
- Pages that make you feel "less than" if you don't own the latest

| Create a peaceful digital space = peaceful financial habits.

4. Apply the 24-Hour Rule

Before buying anything that's not essential, wait 24 hours.
This cools impulse purchases.
You'll often realize: "I don't even want this anymore!"

5. Set Guilt-Free Fun Budgets

You don't have to eliminate fun — just **plan for it**.
-> Example:

- ₹1,000 per month for food delivery
- ₹500 for entertainment or movies

- ₹800 for personal treats

When you spend guilt-free within budget, it feels like **reward, not regret.**

6. Buy Quality, Not Quantity

Sometimes **spending more saves more.**

- Good shoes last 2 years, cheap ones break in 3 months
- One durable water bottle is better than 5 disposables

Long-term cost ↓, satisfaction ↑

7. Celebrate What You're Gaining, Not Losing

Instead of saying:
"I can't eat out this week"
Say:
"I'm choosing to save ₹1,200 for my Goa trip / new phone / emergency fund"

Final Thought:

| "Frugality isn't about having less. It's about making space for what matters most."

You're not depriving yourself — you're **reclaiming control** of your money and your future.

CHAPTER FIVE

SAVE FIRST, SPEND LATER

What Does "Save First, Spend Later" Mean?

Most people follow this broken formula:

| **Earn → Spend → Save what's left** (usually nothing)

But wealthy and financially free people follow this:

| **Earn → Save first → Spend what's left**

It's not about saving what's *leftover*, but about **treating savings as a priority**, not an afterthought.

Why This Rule Changes Everything

1. Builds Financial Discipline Instantly

Saving first turns money management into a habit, not a hope.

When you set aside savings right after income, you automatically adjust your spending to the balance.

Outcome: You live within your means — and grow wealth at the same time.

2. Prevents Lifestyle Inflation

When income increases, most people start:

- Eating out more
- Buying expensive gadgets
- Upgrading cars or phones

But with "save first," your savings increase with income — **not your expenses.**

3. Prepares You for Emergencies

Saved money = peace of mind.

Whether it's job loss, medical bills, or car repairs — you'll be **ready, not ruined.**

| "Emergency fund is your financial seatbelt."

4. Enables Guilt-Free Spending

When you've saved your target amount first, whatever is left can be spent freely.

That's true financial confidence — **joyful, not guilty spending.**

5. Accelerates Your Wealth Goals

- Early saving means:
- More compound interest
- Faster debt freedom
- Earlier financial freedom

How to Apply "Save First, Spend Later" in Daily Life

Step 1: Decide Your Savings Target

Start with **20% of income.** If you earn ₹30,000, save ₹6,000 right away.

Tip: Break savings into clear goals:

- Emergency fund
- SIP/investments
- Future goals (travel, home, etc.)

Step 2: Automate Savings

Set up **auto-debit** to:

- A separate savings account
- Mutual fund SIP
- RD or FD

You won't miss what you don't see.

Step 3: Budget the Rest

Now plan your lifestyle around the **remaining 80%** (not 100%).

- Use the 50-30-20 rule or your custom budget style (covered in earlier posts).

Step 4: Increase Saving % Gradually

Each time your income rises, increase your savings — even by 2–3%.
That's how wealth builds silently and strongly over years.

Remember:

| "The money you save today is the freedom you buy for tomorrow."

CHAPTER SIX

BUILD EMERGENCY FUNDS

What Is an Emergency Fund?

An **emergency fund** is a dedicated amount of money kept aside to cover unexpected and urgent expenses, like:

- Job loss
- Medical emergency
- Sudden repairs (car, home, gadgets)
- Family emergencies

It's NOT meant for:

- Holidays
- Shopping
- Investments

It's your **financial shield** when life surprises you.

Why Emergency Funds Matter So Much

1. Reduces Panic During Crisis

When an emergency strikes, money stress multiplies the crisis. An emergency fund brings peace of mind and time to think clearly.

2. Keeps You Out of Debt

No need to swipe a credit card or borrow at high interest rates. You solve the problem — without building a new one.

3. Protects Your Long-Term Goals

Imagine withdrawing your SIPs or breaking your FD during a crisis. Emergency funds protect your investments from disruption.

4. Builds True Financial Confidence

You're not living paycheck-to-paycheck anymore.
You're saying:

| "I've got this — I'm prepared."

How Much Should You Save?

Minimum: 3 months of essential expenses
Ideal: 6 months or more
Example:
If your monthly needs (rent + bills + groceries + EMI) =   ₹20,000
Then:
Your emergency fund =   ₹60,000 to   ₹1,20,000

How to Build an Emergency Fund — Step-by-Step

1. Start Small, But Start Now

Even saving   ₹1,000/month is better than nothing. Keep increasing gradually.

2. Park It in the Right Place

Best places to keep emergency funds:

- High-interest savings account
- Liquid mutual fund or Flexi FD
- Bank with instant access (avoid locking money in RD/PPF)

| Rule: Safety + Liquidity > Returns

3. Make It Separate from Daily Use

Do not mix with your regular account. Create a **dedicated emergency fund account** — and name it!

Out of sight = Out of temptation
4. *Refill It After Use*
If you ever use it, make it your top priority to **rebuild it.**

Common Mistakes to Avoid

- Using it for planned expenses like weddings or vacations
- Investing it in risky assets (stocks, crypto)
- Thinking you'll "just use credit cards" instead

Remember:

| "If your car needs a spare tire, your life needs a spare fund."

CHAPTER SEVEN

START INVESTING SMARTLY

What Does It Mean to "Invest Smartly"?

Investing smartly isn't about chasing hot stocks or gambling on tips. It's about:

- Making informed decisions
- Choosing the right tools for your goals
- Starting early and staying consistent

Smart investing = **long-term wealth creation with minimum stress**

Why You Must Start Investing (Not Just Saving)

1. Saving = Safety. Investing = Growth

Savings accounts offer 3–4% interest. Inflation eats away your money's value. But investing in smart avenues (like mutual funds, stocks, or gold) gives 8–12% or more.

- ₹10,000/month invested for 15 years = ₹35–40 lakhs
- While just saving it = ₹18 lakhs max

2. The Earlier You Start, The Bigger You Grow

Thanks to **compounding**, your money earns interest — and that interest earns more interest!

- ₹5,000/month for 25 years @12% = ₹1.7 crore
- Start 10 years late? Only ₹50 lakh!

3. Smart Investing Brings Peace of Mind
You won't worry about:

- Retirement
- Children's education
- Emergencies

Because your money is working while you sleep

How to Start Investing Smartly – Step by Step

1. Set Clear Financial Goals
Ask yourself:

- What am I investing for? (Emergency fund, house, retirement, travel?)
- When do I need the money? (Short-term vs long-term)

Smart investing is goal-based, not trend-based.
2. Understand Your Risk Profile
Are you a:

- Conservative investor? (Prefer safety)
- Aggressive investor? (Can handle ups and downs)

Your risk comfort decides your portfolio mix (Equity vs Debt)
3. Start with Beginner-Friendly Tools
Tool/ Description / Ideal For

- Mutual Funds (SIPs) / Professionally managed / Beginners & busy people
- Public Provident Fund (PPF) / 15-year, tax-free / Safe long-term growth
- Index Funds / Low-cost, Nifty, BSE tracking / Smart passive investors
- Digital Gold / Online gold savings / Festive or traditional investors

Start with   ₹500 SIP — consistency beats amount.

4. Use Trusted Platforms

Start with platforms like:

- Groww
- Zerodha Coin
- Paytm Money
- Kuvera
- ET Money

Easy interface
Free demat for mutual funds
Goal-based investing features

5. Avoid These Beginner Mistakes

- Investing based on social media hype
- Checking returns daily
- Skipping research
- Putting all money into one asset

Instead: Be consistent, diversified, and patient.

6. Track and Review Quarterly

- Check if your goals are on track
- Rebalance your portfolio once a year
- Increase SIP when your income increases

Remember:

| "Smart investing is boring. But the results are exciting."

You don't need to be a finance expert — just consistent with basics.

CHAPTER EIGHT

DIVERSIFY YOUR INCOME

In today's uncertain world, relying on just one income source is risky. Whether it's a job or business, anything can change overnight — layoffs, health issues, market crashes, or emergencies. That's why one of the smartest moves toward financial freedom is **diversifying your income.**

What Does It Mean?

To diversify income means to **create multiple sources of money** — so if one stops, the others keep flowing.

Instead of just a salary or one business, you start earning from:

- Side hustles
- Freelancing
- Passive income
- Investments
- Digital products
- Rentals or royalty

Why Is It Important?

1. **Income Stability**: If your job or business stops, your other income sources will support you.

2. **Faster Wealth Building**: Multiple incomes speed up saving, investing, and reaching your financial goals.
3. **Peace of Mind**: You stop living paycheck to paycheck — and start living with confidence.

Real-Life Examples

- A school teacher who also earns through YouTube educational videos
- A salaried employee running an online T-shirt store
- A retired person earning from mutual fund dividends and property rent
- A homemaker writing eBooks and selling them on Amazon KDP

These people have more control, security, and freedom.

How to Start Diversifying Income

1. Skill-Based Freelancing
Write, design, teach, consult, or manage social media — earn on platforms like Fiverr, Upwork, or LinkedIn.

2. Start a Side Business
Sell homemade food, crafts, digital downloads, or resell products online.

3. Create Digital Assets
Write an eBook, build an online course, or start a blog — and earn passive income.

4. Earn from Investments
Start SIPs, buy dividend stocks, or explore REITs and debt funds for regular income.

5. Monetize Hobbies
Turn your passion (music, photography, art) into online gigs or teaching opportunities.

Important Tips

- Start small, stay consistent
- Focus on one stream at a time, then add more

- Don't leave your main income until side income becomes stable
- Learn basic online skills — they open many doors

Final Thought

"Never depend on a single income. Make investment to create a second source."
— Warren Buffett

Diversifying income is not just smart — it's necessary. It gives you freedom, security, and choices. Start now, and grow slowly. The goal is progress, not perfection.

About The Author

Dinesh Sharma Aryal is a finance educator and founder of the Grow Rupees platform. With over 16 years of experience in banking, insurance, and financial markets, Dinesh specializes in making complex financial concepts simple and actionable. His mission is to help individuals build wealth and achieve financial independence with clarity and confidence.

Follow him at Grow Rupees on Facebook for free financial content and tips.

? Connect with the Author

I'd love to hear your feedback and success stories!

? Email: dinesh.sm9@gmail.com

? Website: https://www.growrupees.com

? Facebook: facebook.com/GrowRupees